We the People

The Thirteen Colonies

by Marc Tyler Nobleman

Content Adviser: Julie Richter, Ph.D.,
Independent Scholar and Consultant,
Colonial Williamsburg Foundation

Social Studies Adviser: Professor Sherry L. Field,
Department of Curriculum and Instruction, College of Education,
The University of Texas at Austin

Reading Adviser: Dr. Linda D. Labbo,
Department of Reading Education, College of Education,
The University of Georgia

 COMPASS POINT BOOKS

Minneapolis, Minnesota

The Thirteen Colonies • The Thirteen Colonies • The Thirteen Colon

Photographs ©: North Wind Picture Archives, cover (bottom), 5, 6, 9, 10, 11, 14, 18, 19, 20, 25, 26, 28, 34, 37, 41; Stock Montage, 8, 15, 22, 31, 32, 35; Photri-Microstock, 13; Hulton Getty/Archive Photos, 17, 21, 29, 30, 38.

Editors: E. Russell Primm, Emily J. Dolbear, and Deborah Cannarella
Photo Researchers: Svetlana Zhurkina and Jo Miller
Photo Selector: Linda S. Koutris
Designer: Bradfordesign, Inc.

Library of Congress Cataloging-in-Publication Data

Nobleman, Marc Tyler.
   The thirteen colonies / by Marc Tyler Nobleman.
   p. cm. — (We the people)
   Includes bibliographical references (p.) and index.
 Summary: Introduces the European immigrants who came to North America as explorers and set-
tlers, their interactions with native people, and the wars that ultimately led to their independence.
 ISBN 0-7565-0211-X (hardcover)
 1. United States—History—Colonial period, ca. 1600–1775—Juvenile literature. 2. United
States—Social conditions—To 1865—Juvenile literature. [1. United States—History—Colonial
period, ca. 1600–1775. 2. United States—Social conditions—To 1865.] I. Title. II. We the people
(Compass Point Books)
 E188 .N63 2002
 973.2—dc21   2001004741

TABLE OF CONTENTS

FORTUNE AND FREEDOM

Virginia, Massachusetts, New Hampshire, New York, Maryland, Rhode Island, Connecticut, Delaware, North Carolina, New Jersey, South Carolina, Pennsylvania, and Georgia. These thirteen **colonies** were the first European settlements in North America. To begin with, the thirteen colonies followed the laws of England, but soon the people wanted to make their own laws. In 1776, these colonies became the first thirteen states of the United States of America.

The Europeans wanted colonies in the "New World"—North America, Central America, South America, and the Caribbean—for many reasons. The Spanish were hungry for gold and silver. The French were searching for animals with valuable furs that they could sell. Some of the English people were seeking their fortune in the Americas, too. Most, however, hoped to find freedom—freedom of religion and freedom of government.

4

The Puritans came to North America seeking freedom of religion.

The story of the thirteen colonies is full of fear, bravery, struggle, and luck. It is a tale of adventure, including bold sea voyages, a lost colony, pirates—and even an Indian princess. It was a time of many firsts, from the first Thanksgiving in North America to the founding of the first free country in the world.

5

THE LOST COLONY

In 1585, Sir Walter Raleigh tried to create the first English settlement in North America. He sent a group of 108 people to Roanoke Island, off the coast of what is now the state of North Carolina. Raleigh named the settlement Virginia, in honor of England's Queen Elizabeth I, who was known as the "Virgin Queen." At that time, Virginia stretched along the entire east coast of North America from Canada to Florida.

Sir Walter Raleigh started Roanoke Island, the first English colony in North America.

The living conditions on Roanoke Island were so harsh that the English settlers returned home with Sir Francis Drake in 1586. The

6

colonists had clashed with many of the local Indians, and Drake had warned them that the Spanish might attack them. Then, in 1587, Raleigh sent a second group of more than 100 colonists to the same area. Their leader was John White. About a month after the settlers landed, White's daughter, Eleanor Dare, gave birth to a baby girl. The baby was named Virginia, after the settlement and England's queen. Virginia Dare was the first English child born in the Americas.

Something mysterious happened on Roanoke Island. White left his family and the other settlers there when he sailed back to England in August 1587 to get more supplies. A war between England and Spain in 1588 kept White from returning to Virginia until 1590. When he finally arrived back at the settlement, he discovered that the colonists—and almost all trace of them—had disappeared. The only clue to what had happened to them was the word *Croatoan* carved into a tree. *Croatoan* was the name of a friendly group of Indians and the Indian name for a nearby island. White could not search the small island because of bad weather. The fate of the Lost

Colony is still unknown. Some historians believe the colonists simply moved away. Others think they were killed by Indians.

The English did not give up the idea of settling Virginia—but they waited almost seventeen years before they tried again. In 1607, England's King James I gave two English companies the right to settle Virginia. The Virginia Company of Plymouth tried to settle northern Virginia but did not succeed. The Virginia Company of London, however, settled in southern Virginia. Jamestown, Virginia, was the first permanent English settlement in the Americas. It was also the first of the thirteen American colonies.

John White returned to Roanoke Island in 1590 to find that the colony had been abandoned.

8

JAMESTOWN, VIRGINIA

The Virginia Company sent 104 men and boys to a woodland near Chesapeake Bay in Virginia. The settlers built a fort surrounded by a fence made of wooden stakes to protect themselves from attack by Indians. They named their small colony "Jamestown" in honor of the king.

King James I encouraged the first permanent English settlement in North America.

    The colonists found it difficult to live in the wilderness, however. The area they settled was swampy and swarming with mosquitoes. Summers were too hot, and winters were too cold. None of the settlers knew how to farm, so they could not plant the crops they needed for food. Within a few months after set-

9

tling Jamestown, more than half of the men died of starvation or disease.

Without John Smith, Jamestown probably would not have survived. Smith was a hard worker, and he expected everyone else to work hard, too. He told the men that they wouldn't eat if they didn't work. Smith knew that the colonists could learn a lot from the Indians in the region, but the Indians were cautious about the strange newcomers. He tried to create a friendly relationship between the native people and the settlers.

Captain John Smith was the leader of the Jamestown Colony

Smith kept a journal describing his experiences. He wrote that the Indian chief Powhatan had ordered his warriors to kill Smith. But Powhatan's thirteen-year-old daughter, the Indian princess Pocahontas, asked her father to spare Smith's life, and Smith was not killed. Powhatan and his tribe then became friends with Smith and the settlers.

The Indians taught Smith and the other settlers how to fish and hunt. They also taught the settlers how to grow corn, which became an important food for the settlers. People in England knew that life in the new colony was hard, but more settlers arrived in 1608 and 1609. In 1609, John Smith was wounded by an accidental explosion of gunpowder and had to return to England. On his return venture in 1614, he mapped and named the coast of New England.

Pocahontas begged Powhatan to save John Smith's life.

11

The winter of 1609–1610 was so harsh that the colonists called it the "starving time." Some of them were so desperate that they abandoned the other settlers and went to live with the Indians. Many people in Jamestown died. When John Smith left, just six months earlier, 500 people lived in the settlement. When new settlers arrived in 1610, they found that only sixty people had survived the winter.

By 1614, life in Jamestown had improved. John Rolfe taught the colonists how to grow a plant called tobacco. The smoking of tobacco leaves was popular in London. The settlers sold their crop at high prices and many of them became wealthy. They created large tobacco farms, called plantations, throughout Virginia. The tobacco farmers took much of this land from the Indians, however. They damaged the good relationship that John Smith had formed with the native people.

The plantation owners now needed more people to work in the tobacco fields. They paid for poor people to

John Rolfe and other settlers grew tobacco in Jamestown.

travel from Europe. These Europeans worked as **indentured servants** for several years, hoping that one day they would own their own land. Some plantation workers did not come to the Americas of their own free will, however.

In 1619, a Dutch ship arrived in Jamestown from western Africa. The people on board that ship had been kidnapped from their homelands in Africa by slave traders. They were sold to the plantation owners in the Americas as

13

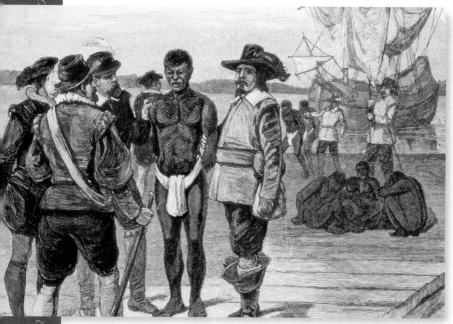

Dutch ships brought the first African slaves into the Virginia colony.

slaves and servants. Unlike the servants from Europe, the Africans could never earn their freedom. They would be slaves for the rest of their lives. The slave labor in Virginia marked the beginning of slavery in the United States, perhaps the most shameful development in American history. In 1641, Massachusetts was the first colony in North America to establish slavery, and Connecticut legalized slavery in 1650. Virginia formally established slavery in 1662.

Another historic event took place in Jamestown in 1619, but it was positive. An assembly called the House of Burgesses was formed. Its members were elected by the

14

male landowners of Jamestown and its purpose was to make laws. Women at the time did not have the right to vote. The House of Burgesses was the first representative government by Europeans in North America. A representative government **represents** the wishes and ideas of the people who are ruled by it. The young colony of Virginia had planted the seeds of a new nation.

The Virginia House of Burgesses was the first representative government in North America.

PLYMOUTH, MASSACHUSETTS

The people who established the second English settlement in America were called the Pilgrims. The word *pilgrim* means "homeless wanderer." These people came to America because they wanted to be free to worship as they wished.

The official religion in England at that time was the Church of England, also known as the Anglican Church. The king did not allow the people to follow any other religion. People who did not follow the Church of England were put in prison or sent out of the country. Sometimes they were killed.

Some members of the Anglican Church were called Puritans. These people had different ideas about the Anglican Church than the king did. They tried to change the church rituals, but King James I would not allow them to express their ideas. Some of the Puritans, who were called Pilgrims, decided to leave England to find religious freedom.

16

First they went
to the Netherlands.
Then they wanted to
live in a new country,
a country of their
own. In 1620, forty-
one Pilgrims left the
Netherlands to go to
North America.
Sixty-one other peo-
ple traveled with the

The Puritans wanted England's King James I to change church rituals, but he refused.

Pilgrims. The Pilgrims called their traveling companions
the Strangers because they were not a part of their church.
Some Strangers hoped to find adventure and riches. Others
were military officers in charge of protecting the group.
One of these officers was Captain Miles Standish.

The Pilgrims and the Strangers left in September
1620. They traveled from Plymouth, England, to the
Americas on a ship called the *Mayflower*. The stormy and

The Pilgrims and the Strangers sailed from England to Massachusetts on the Mayflower.

dangerous voyage across the ocean took more than two months. In November, the group landed in Provincetown on the tip of Cape Cod, Massachusetts. *Massachusetts* is an Indian word that means "at the big hill." In December, they moved farther down the coast and settled in a place they named Plymouth.

Within days after they arrived on Cape Cod, the group made a written agreement. They agreed that they would work together for peace and freedom in their new settlement. They agreed that they would make their own laws, and that everyone would follow them—both Pilgrims and Strangers. The settlers called this agreement the Mayflower Compact. One of the men who helped write the

18

Mayflower Compact was William Bradford. William Brewster, the Pilgrim's religious leader, died soon after the group arrived. Bradford then became the new leader and the governor of Plymouth.

Like the settlers in Jamestown, the settlers in Plymouth suffered during a severe first winter. Almost half of the 102 members of the colony died. In the spring of 1621, the leader of the Pemaquid Indian tribe offered to help the Pilgrims. His name was Samoset. The settlers were surprised that Samoset spoke English. The Indian had learned the language from the English explor-

The settlers in Massachusetts signed the Mayflower Compact, agreeing to work together and obey the colony's new laws.

19

The settlers in Plymouth established a peace treaty with Chief Massasoit.

ers who had traveled through the region.

Samoset introduced the settlers to Squanto, an Indian from the Pawtuxet tribe. Squanto taught them how to fish and how to plant corn, beans, and other crops. Samoset also introduced them to Massasoit, the chief of the Wampanoag tribe. The colonists and Massasoit made a treaty, or agreement, to live in peace. Their treaty lasted fifty years.

Because the Indians had taught them to grow their own food, the colonists had many crops that year. In October, to celebrate the great harvest, the settlers invited the Indians to a three-day feast. This celebration is now considered the first Thanksgiving celebration in North America. The colonists and the Indians ate deer, duck,

20

geese, turkey, clams, fish, corn bread, and many kinds of vegetables, including pumpkins.

In 1630, many more Puritans left England to find religious freedom in North America. That year, Boston was founded. Today, Boston is the capital of the state of Massachusetts. Harvard College, the first institution of higher learning in the Americas, was founded in the area in 1636. By 1640, 20,000 colonists had settled in New England. In 1691, Plymouth, Boston, and other nearby settlements became part of the Massachusetts Bay Colony.

The Pilgrims and Indians celebrated the first Thanksgiving in 1621.

21

THE NEW ENGLAND COLONIES

Four of the thirteen original colonies were settled in a section of North America known as New England. The first such colony was Massachusetts. The others were New Hampshire, Rhode Island, and Connecticut.

In the 1620s, King James I gave some land in North America to two friends, John Mason and Ferdinando Gorges. In 1629, the two men divided their large piece of land at the Piscataqua River. Gorges claimed the land east of the river while Mason claimed the

King James I gave land to two friends.

land to the west. Mason's piece of land was called New

This map shows the original thirteen colonies.

Hampshire. Some people believe that Mason named it
after the English county of Hampshire where he had lived.
Others believe that John Smith named New Hampshire
while he was exploring the coast of New England several

23

years earlier. Gorges' area remained part of Massachusetts until 1820, when it became Maine.

In 1636, some Puritans began to leave Massachusetts. Many settled in New Hampshire, while some traveled to other regions. Some of these people wanted fertile farmland. Others were still looking for religious freedom. The Pilgrims had left England because they wanted freedom of religion, but some Puritans in Massachusetts did not accept people who did not share their beliefs.

Roger Williams was a Puritan minister in Boston, Massachusetts. He believed that the Puritans should allow other people to follow their own religions. He also said that Indians should be paid for their land. Many people did not like Williams because of his ideas. Massachusetts Governor John Winthrop wanted to send him back to England. Before Winthrop could act, however, Williams left Boston in the middle of winter. For more than three months, he lived in the woods. The

Narragansett In-
dians who lived in
the region helped
Williams survive.

In 1636,
Williams and some
of his followers
founded Providence,
Rhode Island, near
Narragansett Bay.

The unpopular Puritan minister Roger Williams left Massachusetts in 1635.

The name *Rhode Island* may have come from Dutch words
meaning "red island," because there was red clay in the area.
Others believe that an Italian explorer named the region after
the Greek island of Rhodes. The new colony was a true **haven**
of religious freedom. People of all faiths were welcomed
there—Puritans, Roman Catholics, Jews, and Quakers (also
called the Society of Friends).

In 1636, Thomas Hooker, another Puritan minister, also
left Massachusetts. He led a group of supporters to rich farm-

land along the shores of a wide, long river. There, Hooker founded the town of Hartford. Soon, the settlements of Hartford, Windsor, and Wethersfield united to form the colony of Connecticut. The name *Connecticut* is a Mohican Indian word meaning "at the long tidal river."

In 1639, Connecticut became the first colony with a written plan of government. The plan was called the Fundamental Orders of Connecticut. This plan called for the election of a governor and meetings of lawmakers, but it did not include the English king. Connecticut was going to govern itself. Thomas Hooker is sometimes called the "father of American democracy."

Thomas Hooker and other Puritan settlers established the town of Hartford along the Connecticut River.

26

THE MIDDLE ATLANTIC COLONIES

The Middle Atlantic colonies included New York, Maryland, Delaware, New Jersey, and Pennsylvania. Some of these areas had first been claimed by Dutch and Swedish settlers. The English took over these regions, however, and formed their own colonies.

In 1624, Dutch settlers from the Netherlands founded a settlement along the Hudson River. The river was named for Henry Hudson, an English explorer who had visited the region in 1609. The Dutch settlement was called New Netherland. Its central town was New Amsterdam, named for the Dutch city of Amsterdam.

New Amsterdam was founded on Manhattan Island in 1626. The Dutch governor, Peter Minuit, had given the Indians some cloth, beads, and other goods in exchange for the island. The goods were worth about 60 Dutch guilders, or 2,400 English cents (which may be why, today, we remember the price as U.S. $24). Indians did not believe that land could be owned by people. They probably did not realize that the Dutch were trying to buy the island. They may have considered the deal a loan, but not a purchase.

In 1638, settlers from Sweden founded New Sweden. In 1655, the Dutch claimed New Sweden and made it part of New Netherland. The Swedish settlement did not last long, but its settlers played an important part in American history. They built the first log cabins in the Americas.

Peter Minuit, a Dutch settler, purchased Manhattan Island from the Indians for about $24.

In 1664, the English took New Netherland from the Dutch without firing a shot. The English renamed the region New York, in honor of James, the Duke of York and the brother of King Charles II.

Like the New England colonies, Maryland was founded by English settlers who wanted religious freedom. In 1632, King Charles I gave Sir George Calvert some land in North America. Sir Calvert was known as the first Lord of Baltimore. Calvert's son, Cecil, founded Maryland as a haven for Roman Catholics. Another son,

Sir George Calvert was the first Lord of Baltimore.

Leonard, led the first group from England to the new colony. Leonard became the first governor of Maryland.

Today, the city of Baltimore is the largest city in the state of Maryland.

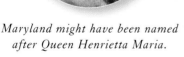

Some historians believe Maryland was named for Queen Henrietta Maria, the Roman Catholic wife of King Charles I. Others believe the settlement was named for Mary, the woman Christians believe was the mother of Jesus Christ. In 1649, Maryland passed the first toleration act in the colonies. This law granted religious freedom, but only to Christians (people who believe that Jesus Christ is **divine**). People of other beliefs could stay in Maryland only if they kept quiet.

Maryland might have been named after Queen Henrietta Maria.

Some of the region that had been New Sweden later

became Delaware and New Jersey. Delaware was named after Lord De La Warr, a governor of Jamestown, Virginia. The Duke of York gave part of the land to his friend Sir George Carteret. This land was named New Jersey in Carteret's honor. Carteret had been governor of Jersey, one of England's Channel Islands.

In 1681, King Charles II wanted to repay a debt to a friend who had died. He gave a large piece of land in North America to his friend's son, William Penn. The king renamed the area *Pennsylvania*, which means "Penn's woods."

Penn was a Quaker. The Quakers believe that all people—of every religion, race, and gender—are

William Penn received land from the king to establish a colony in Pennsylvania.

31

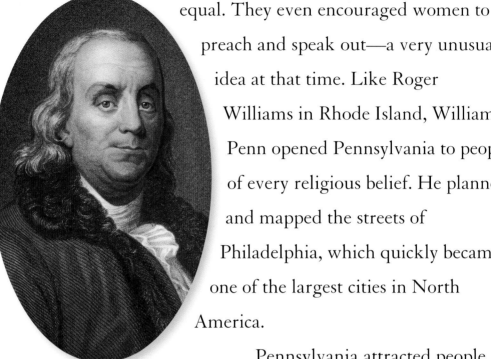

Benjamin Franklin lived much of his life in Philadelphia.

equal. They even encouraged women to preach and speak out—a very unusual idea at that time. Like Roger Williams in Rhode Island, William Penn opened Pennsylvania to people of every religious belief. He planned and mapped the streets of Philadelphia, which quickly became one of the largest cities in North America.

Pennsylvania attracted people from all over Europe. German, Scottish, and French settlers came to the colony. Many Indians who had been forced out of their native homelands also settled there. A boy from Boston came, too. His name was Benjamin Franklin. He would grow up to do many great things for the thirteen colonies. He also became one of the Founding Fathers of the United States of America.

THE SOUTHERN COLONIES

Virginia was the first of the thirteen English colonies—and the first southern colony. The other southern colonies were North Carolina, South Carolina, and Georgia.

In 1663, King Charles II granted land in North America to eight English lords. The land was originally called Carolina in honor of King Charles I (*Carolus* is the Latin word for "Charles"). Soon, Carolina was divided into North Carolina and South Carolina. Between 1650 and 1653, people from Virginia and other colonies began to settle in North Carolina. In 1670, the busy seaport of Charles Town, South Carolina, was founded. Its name was changed to Charleston in 1718.

The Carolinas soon became famous for rice and indigo—a plant that produces a blue dye. North Carolina was also famous for something much more frightening—pirates! The fierce British pirate known as Blackbeard, whose real name was Edward Teach, hid out in the colony after robbing

33

Blackbeard, a fierce pirate, lived in North Carolina.

ships of their treasure. Blackbeard was killed by a lieutenant from Virginia in 1718.

In 1732, James Oglethorpe founded the last of the thirteen original colonies. He named it Georgia, in honor of King George II. Oglethorpe founded the colony for people who were going to prison. In Britain at that time, people who could not pay their debts were sent to jail. The jails were called debtors' prisons, and the prisoners were treated badly. Oglethorpe thought the debtors should work on their own farms in Georgia. This way, they could make the money they needed to pay their debts—which they could never do if they were in prison.

Oglethorpe's idea was a good one, but it didn't work. Many debtors thought that life in prison would be better than life in the wilderness of Georgia, and they refused to leave England. Many of those who did settle in Georgia did not want to work on the farms—they wanted slaves to do the work for them. Georgia also had trouble with Indians, pirates, and other colonists. The region bordered the British colony of South Carolina and the Spanish colony of Florida. Many battles between the British and the Spanish were fought on Georgia's soil.

James Oglethorpe founded Georgia in 1732.

TIME FOR CHANGE

From the late 1600s to the mid-1700s, wars raged over ownership of the colonies. Battles between Britain and France (sometimes with Spain) were fought in Europe and North America. The fourth and final of these wars was known in the colonies as the French and Indian War (1754–1763). Various Indian tribes fought on both sides. In 1763, Britain won the war and took control of all French lands. Now, however, Britain needed more money to pay for the war and to settle and protect its new land.

To get the money, King George III began to add taxes to the price of glass, paper, tea, paint, and other goods. This meant that the colonists had to pay the king a fee for many of the things they bought from Britain. Britain also tried to keep the colonists from making certain items themselves. The colonists were angry. They did not feel it was right for Britain to tax them without their approval. If they were going to be ruled by Britain, they

During the French and Indian War, Britain fought France for control of the North American colonies.

37

On December 16, 1773, colonists in Boston, Massachusetts,
protested the British tax on tea by dumping tea into the Charles River.

38

felt that they should have a say in the British government. To show their anger, they decided to **boycott** goods from Britain. The king grew angry, too, and raised the taxes.

Tensions grew between the people of the colonies and the British rulers. As the colonists became stronger and more independent, Britain tried harder to keep them under control. Many colonists no longer felt connected to the country that they or their relatives had left years before. Some had never even seen it. Soon, the colonists demanded a change. They no longer wanted to obey British laws. The colonists no longer wanted to be part of Britain. They wanted to rule themselves.

"FREE AND INDEPENDENT"

In 1700, the population of the thirteen colonies had been about 400,000. By 1775, it was 2.5 million and included many great leaders such as George Washington and Thomas Jefferson. Both of these men were born in the first colony—Virginia.

In 1775, war broke out between Britain and the colonies. The first shots of the Revolutionary War were fired in Lexington and Concord, Massachusetts. One year later, on July 4, 1776, the colonists approved the Declaration of Independence. This famous document, written by Thomas Jefferson, gave the thirteen colonies a new name: "the United States of America."

In 1783, the Revolutionary War officially ended. The colonists had finally won the freedom they had been seeking when they came to the Americas. They had arrived as English settlers, but from now on, they would be Americans. The thirteen original colonies had become the first thirteen "free and independent" states of a new nation.

By the 1770s, people living in the thirteen colonies did not want to be ruled by Britain any longer. They wanted to create their own country.

41

GLOSSARY

boycott—to refuse to buy something

colonies—lands settled by people from another country and ruled by that country

divine—holy; sacred

haven—a safe place

indentured servant—a person who must work for someone for a certain amount of time to repay travel and other expenses

represents—speaks or acts for someone else

DID YOU KNOW?

- The first flag of the United States was called the Stars and Stripes. It had thirteen stripes and thirteen stars—one star and one stripe for each of the thirteen colonies.

- The Indian princess Pocahontas had three names. Her real name was Matoaka, which means "little snow feather." Her nickname, Pocahontas, means "playful one." She got this name because she would often do cartwheels in the middle of Jamestown. When she married John Rolfe, she was called Lady Rebecca.

- The Great Seal of the United States has thirteen stars and an eagle wearing a shield of thirteen stripes and holding thirteen arrows. The seal is printed on the U.S. $1 bill.

IMPORTANT DATES

Timeline

1620	The Pilgrims leave Plymouth, England, and settle in Plymouth, Massachusetts.
1634	The Calverts settle Maryland.
1636	Roger Williams settles Rhode Island; Thomas Hooker settles Connecticut.
1664	The English take New Netherland from the Dutch. It becomes New York, New Jersey, and Delaware.
1670	Charleston, South Carolina, is founded.
1681	King Charles II gives William Penn a large piece of land, which he names Pennsylvania.
1691	The Massachusetts Bay Colony is formed.
1732	James Oglethorpe settles Georgia.
1775	The Revolutionary War begins.
1776	The colonists approve the Declaration of Independence.
1783	The Revolutionary War ends.

IMPORTANT PEOPLE

THOMAS HOOKER

(1586–1647), *Puritan minister who founded Hartford, Connecticut*

JAMES OGLETHORPE

(1696–1785), *founder of Georgia*

WILLIAM PENN

(1644–1718), *Quaker leader who founded Pennsylvania*

SIR WALTER RALEIGH

(1552? –1618), *explorer who named Virginia and tried to establish the first English settlement there*

JOHN SMITH

(1580–1631), *leader of the settlement in Jamestown, Virginia, who also explored and named New England*

ROGER WILLIAMS

(1603?–1683), *founder of the colony of Rhode Island, a haven of religious freedom*

WANT TO KNOW MORE?

At the Library

Coleman, Brooke. *Roanoke: The Lost Colony.* New York: PowerKids Press, 2000.

Hakim, Joy. *Making Thirteen Colonies.* New York: Oxford University Press, 1999.

Isaacs, Sally Senzell. *America in the Time of Pocahontas: 1590 to 1754.* Chicago: Heinemann Library, 2001.

Sakurai, Gail. *The Thirteen Colonies.* New York: Children's Press, 2000.

On the Web

For more information on the *thirteen colonies,* use FactHound

to track down Web sites related to this book.

1. Go to *http://www.compasspointbooks.com/facthound*

2. Type in this book ID: 075650211X

3. Click on the *Fetch It* button.

Your trusty FactHound will fetch the best Web sites for you!

Through the Mail

National Archives and Records Administration

Archives 1 Research Support Branch (NWCC1)

Room 406

700 Pennsylvania Avenue, N.W.

Washington, DC 20408-0001

To request copies of important documents and symbols, such as the Declaration of Independence and the Great Seal of the United States

On the Road

Williamsburg, Virginia

800/HISTORY

http://www.history.org

To experience life in the living, working city of Colonial Williamsburg

Plimouth Plantation

P.O. Box 1620

Plymouth, MA 02362

508/746-1622

To visit the living history museum in Plymouth, Massachusetts, and step aboard a reproduction of the *Mayflower*, the ship on which the Pilgrims traveled to the Americas

INDEX

About the Author

Marc Tyler Nobleman has written eight books for young readers. He has also written for *The Great American History Quiz*, a History Channel program, and for several children's magazines, including *Highlights for Children*. Additionally, he is a cartoonist, and his single panels have appeared in more than forty magazines.